I0151446

Pinch the Lock

poems by

Candice Louisa Daquin

Finishing Line Press
Georgetown, Kentucky

Pinch the Lock

Publisher: Leah Maines

Editor: Christen Kincaid

Cover Art: AdobeStock_59128476.jpeg

Author Photo: Candice Louisa Daquin

Cover Design: Elizabeth Maines McCleavy

Printed in the USA on acid-free paper.
Order online: www.finishinglinepress.com
also available on amazon.com

Author inquiries and mail orders:
Finishing Line Press
P. O. Box 1626
Georgetown, Kentucky 40324
U. S. A.

Table of Contents

When you stop and empty yourself

Empty yourself
like a full bag
falling out in pieces
here the lipstick
here the soul
we lie in wait
for our time
expecting miracles to pluck us
like glowing robin
bright in white ice

behind the facade
carried wool, leather, metal,
wooden effigies
multifaceted
multifaceted masks

we tremble
like snow rabbit with black tail
seen by high bird of prey
hiding behind rock, shakes
sloths off danger, makes heartfelt
race, hop; hop
the shadow defending
our fear is in never knowing
how it will end

empty yourself
old hair brush
half eaten snack
pressed violet between book
storing faintly, yourself within yourself
retrieved among debris
still flowing with hope

so we gather young sentiment
rush pathways with our run
frankincense following
this year will
find our tithe within
the story
of
ourselves
long carried
rarely delved

1

Penance

You there
in the corner
have you paid yet?
hitch hikers are prohibited
dreamers need not apply
life's for those who are
exquisitely trained
in kissing the ring
on bended knee
penance child
learned sharp and early
when wonderment
banished to toy chest
is replaced by rote
wake up, eat, compliment the boss
climb into your cubicle
and should
the red hue of a fallen leaf
capture your straying scream
Penance shall
with her devouring rod
scour your wandering heart
tying fancies to stones
overboard thrown
no room for questions
here is your date
neat and prickly
faintly you are
through misted glass
child
run
run fast
lest you be
sucked up
your imaginings
ground to
dust

Woolen masks

When the revolution came
we wore masks of wool
high socks and shoes of leaves
by then see, their secret was out
and we'd joined sides with the trees

Practice fuck

She was
the girl they
learned to fuck on
nothing more

a rubber doll
malleable parts
watching their looks of
concentration
as practicing
they honed their art

obligingly she
opened her legs
offered a breast
all the while feeling nothing
of their divining rod
rooting for gold
in supplied loin

her insides on loan
half instructor
half whore
they drooled words of love
as climaxing on her
they learned how
to pleasure themselves
anew, without furtive hand or
well-thumbed magazine

how she learned her role
so skillful, when pressed to
mount, obligingly spread or
submissively suck, she played
her part immaculately
teaching these fools to be
a little less clumsy, sloppy
too fast, wrong hole, right froth

all the while they mined depths
not once caring for her pleasure
in youthful spurt, mounting often
working out how to maximize
through repetition, their eyes
rolled back in dream, she
often wondered when learned
who eventually they'd use their skills upon

and if, when showing off
they'd ever give thought again to
a girl of seventeen
tired and sore from being
a practice fuck for
hormone and boys with hard
hearts

Whispers in the dust

Don't mock my flat chest or empty stomach
we didn't eat for years when we crossed the desert
our people were left as crystalized markers
sand blown to glass
a woman holding a baby
a child bending to pick up a mirage
we died in crystal and came back in dune
high and mighty, wind swept in regret
they chased us until the horses ate death
and soon the only sign we existed
marks in the sand, an outstretched hand
slow footprints of the dammed
who sought refuge and found only
starvation and quiet loss
we ceased being human and became
whispers in the dust

Reincarnation

It isn't sufficient
to be nice or even fair
sometimes the train to equality
is bent to outdo, thrive, push, push, be the best
and I have fallen weary of that fight tonight
where not long before
a city shook with new violence, old ideals, emptied streets, jammed
phones, get away screams

reminding me of why I
threw the towel in
used the last rations of sanity
to get here
where by desert moon
we are all still
jack rabbit, armadillo and wildling kestrel
a moment as we feel beneath us
our shared earth gurgle

asked if I miss the city,
a marmalade of lights,
stock answer comes easy, but
if I strip off my fear and leave the suit here
walk deep into cacti
drink from the root
I'll say the same on my return

twice buried, twice burned
if we need speak at all
for combining with stars
I see an advantage to silence
brushing over prairie grass turning mauve with drought as we humans
taint water with our thirst

oh to be still
see a different light
blinking down from expansive universe
I am reminded when I died
woke no longer needing to scale
those heights

my new life sets
with red braids of bright
I bury my former deep in cinnamon earth
that one day
she might be born again from husk of old
like desert fox, slim and muscular, makes her escape
over hills, down into velvet keep, enfolding
songs of animal and human in burgundy sleep

Three young men on a train

Who of these brave men?
knew of their launch when
aboard rushing train
terrorism strikes sulphur
in butterflies' vein

faces cauterized in shock
with fires resinous dew upon their loath
calling hoarse into fog
who shall without much decision
nimble cessation of self
released like oiled spring
give away safety and surge
a danger beyond horror
plunging into ice
thwarting usual dying
to save
when all around
peace is burning
set high in erasing hill
darkened by evolution
of emergent sin,
specter in foreign land

attacks sudden, sharp,
like Christmas cracker
flinging contents in gasp
you men of olden valor
may not know what metal makes
your souls, till tested you
leave aside safest path
unbidden, rush the monster
in countless spontaneous
bloom, saving lives in
ready reach
arcing time and history

this remembered reflecting
poem is for you
when called
who act and save
by rare conscience
we lose in fault
for greatest acts are
those unasked for
sudden in resolutions
watchful
courage

Scar

She said
don't be mad
but you have scars on your back
and as the paint of forty dried
I learned something new
you can fall from horses
even in sleep
where maybe in absinthe dream we met
by starlight
indistinct
yet you know my shape
from other times
when I was not myself

and you
you were always there

a whisper of conscience
a ribbon around my wrist
falling in equal weight
we are born again and again
sometimes you are a bird
and I the tree, you the land
to keep watch

next time
write your memories for me
in dark pearls
lost in sand
coming up as moon
forged in silver trees

Substance

Exist in me
long after
taking final, sonorous breath
heavy with fluttering
glial of death
husky in her beckon
reaching deeper eventual

exist in me
though time took
you in physic
leaching whisper from
wet cry
not yet
not ever
you are mine
we fall and rise
elements of surge

exist in me
when I have dissolved
in distilled space, that former
spark run through keeping
charge, brightens in absence
lighthouse lamp

exist
in
me
fetch from dark all
carved creation
mortal machination
that substance
not found in myself
without your
guide
sweeping like
aching fingers
across map
of who I am

Pornography

Slapping blood suckers
take a ticket
seats are sticky
we wait in mortuary grey
birds clack against glass
air conditioning on high
large, sweating bodies
confined and fidgeting in place
the flick of homemade fan
a much pawed magazine
smell of cherry coke
a baby suckling
life and death in marital vows

she wears red
he selects the mistress
scolds hymen her tight mistrust
honeymoon disease a topic of
gossip among white haired men
reminiscent of when
they nailed a virgin to the door
left her spread open like a pinned butterfly
running tears of silver from her wedding gown
life between her legs already crawling
no time to mend, bend your knee
crouch for the wafer, suck his demands, birth sons not daughter's

unstuck I leave my clothes on the lions chair
spread myself thin as old men reach and stare
we're emancipated women
and you, with your vermin ways
masturbating to girls while weary wife cooks and slaves
take a look
lean in deep
you'll never get any
not a piece of me
I'm free of being
a page out of your pornography

Corn maiden

What does the child think?
a color in homogeneous corn
streaking tears
feeling sting
of father's hand
get away
my enemy is my friend
blood doesn't turn
hate to kin

she reveals like pickled ginger
pink and thin, her stung skin
inspecting weekly
worn over with corn husk
turn to dust
this crop circle

first betrayal
escapes burned flesh
that empty feeling
not part of this
find your own
clan
where in land
rugged, unknowing, unwelcome
doors shut
no room here
child
keep walking
knock on the door least opened
find yourself inside
a corn maiden of turquoise
rolling in moon light like cats eyes

Lighthouse

Through layers
sweater, vest, coat
skin somewhere beneath
lost to clothes
cold in swept plains
diving middle country
with frosted gallop
unexploded

her small eyes
almost oriental with age
Nordic cheeks
arising with frost
I fling my stick arms
pinched by fabric
we hug far apart
she nearly cries

I see years of knowing
memories written on her face instead of lines
with old friends who carry
snow globes of
inside jokes
vignettes of shared past
pulling stitches tighter

so we last
in spite of contrary ways and lazy checks
anger fading in familiarity
like a hand on my shoulder
caring without label

she leaves
close doors against night chill
misting windows
a fairy world
she's driving off
I feel a light pull
like spindle unraveling
leading thread from her life to mine
keeping watch
lighthouses are not just for sailors
blind to shore

Mother

The girl inside
never grows tired
of resting her ghost head
in imagined rest
on her
mothers lap

even when sizzling, she leaves in reduction
cold her shadow stretches
and house is still
in staid drowsy sleep
you long yet
what you may not have
unable to replicate
your mother's enveloped being
in that moment
dwelling close
filling you with
familiar eyes

regret has earned wings
shake this aching sting
her arms covering
In touching pollinated ground
merging
where did I start?
you begin
so our blood swims
if you are walking swallow footed
with me or apart
despite or because
we live in each other's
life force

Avalanche

Winter
in all your unfurled sympathy
left white dreams
lying in trees
we hear our breath
sharp in cold
a purity
as tramping hard
downturned against wind
chins tucked in
we climb hills
Winter
with your imagined ice palate
resting storms in sky like
unfinished thoughts
pinch none awake
to passion
breathed out hot
against pine filled roads
you take my hand
rubbing it
our energies sparking
I hold myself steady
against avalanche
thinking
this must be
the feeling
they talk about

Repulsion

I was 17 when I first
watched Repulsion
Catherine Deneuve
too beautiful
for objectivity
if she wasn't believable
her icy perfection
magnified slow
creep of madness
descending into empty
apartment echoing with
imagined voices
whispering from
other side

don't forget to
stitch her up
when she stabs herself

I held an idea
beauty and madness
were necessary for each other

when I felt myself
unraveling into
separate spindles
cold water spilling
from porcelain
mist on flat earth
like exhaustion
vaporizing in
torn hiss

I took care to wear
a clean dress
though it
was too cold
to properly
wash
my hair

Pinch the lock

Oh no
that pinched bird face
staring back
it isn't the real you

oh no
the real you
runs with unimaginably long skirts
slides down stairs
claps with castanets on her wrists
gypsy verse inhabiting your soul

oh no
you are not that woman
fitful of herself
applying salve to broken smile
sleeping at night on blue pills
and tied back jowls

oh no
the real you
wears gold bikini, deep sea diving
makes love at 2am without care for consequence
rattles cages, freeing those pinched faced birds
who, unable to fly, forgot they were avian
and stared into mirrors with pecked expression

oh no
like a carpet of color they release
you hear the sound of a hundred latches falling back
empty of prisoner
pretty cage
pretty display

oh no
better to flock
rising ever higher
in amused drift
on warm wind
carrying you further
than you've ever
dared

Dune

I ride out to where noise
if there is a barrier
separating human din from
unending space
meets

it is a day of long shadows
and emptied carcasses
stuffing roadsides
like marbles
husks of
armadillo, deer, antelope

and maybe in that list
myself
rolling with dust
changing color
turkey buzzards swell above
brief flashes of wing
ragged and immense
dwarfing our little pursuits

we are only
rats in suits
mounting absurdity
tipping the hamster wheel
with glut and gloat

these arcing creatures
they know
living isn't free
or easy
you lie dying
and they survive
carrying you away
until
husk of shell
you resemble
glass
shining in
setting red sun
against emptiness everywhere
rolling inside you
never so filled
with life

Marriage

Whatsoever lies beneath
two people
in slow tree ring of union
whatsoever lurks between
a marriage
built on kindling from
green willow
this hastily made stick house
must endure first winter's
tempestuous yang

we carry heavier load
as spring brings yang
wood felled in cry
becomes timber to keep
two people dry
still it leaks
wind and gale
reminding us
it is the frailty
of trust
thin as mist
that must, us, last

until thaw
when together we
dry bricks in sun
place them
frame our home
facing future's fissures
in solid foundation
for those days
living on see-saw
watching waves gather high
on life's shirred shore

I know in our hands
coming together
hazelnut halves
we brace ourselves
twice betwixt us
mortar & miter
forever

that is how
through smallest things
a
marriage
lasts

For the mothers who should not have died

How much more do you want?
I gave you my pound of flesh
you dissected what had been private
laying it on stainless steel table
emptied me of female parts
sewed up and crossed your fingers

why do we mothers, wives, girls, women of war?
go again and again
lopping of breasts
genitals
wombs
poisoned by this loom of life
woven in metal and cutting deep
submit to butcher
take a ticket
forgo shame
spread your secrets

we birth your babies
wipe up miscarriages
suck out mistakes
stitch up home spun
attempt to escape
our lyre of love
listless in skin
wax fire molten
mannequin without mouth

why did I die?
when I've yet to be heard?
said the tired lady in her bed
listening to her husband
curse at wooden God
why did I die?

when there's so much left to live?
said the spirit leaving her body
wrapped in frankincense and saffron mist
her children place flowers
that unwanted, prematurely wither
oh! Keep me from witnessing my own death!
she whispers to storming skies
If it must come
let me be running

barefoot
staining my feet
with blueberries
bewitched by first sun
pouring like condensed cream
into my outstretched arms
let me hear bird song and
the purr of my cat
stretching from sleep

and
when it is my time
do not savage me
clinically
piece by piece
in steel bed
with weeping floor

no
I am not here
I have
run
laughing
the may pole
Queen
trailing
flowers
out the door

Little boy

You have to see it from my perspective
I'm a Cubano
my parents came here, now I speak French
we talk about hockey, timetables, future careers
they study at night and nobody celebrates
the saints feasts with tears and cakes anymore
everyone is serious, like puppets with marionette lines dragging their
smiles from their faces
discussing white-things like white-people
forgetting the colors of their dreams

but I am nine and I want to play
so when you come to me
bearing gifts
forgive me for my disinterest and desire
to watch football instead of you
with your big green eyes dripping with good intention
wanting to cut up napkins
and make snowflakes and people holding hands

I can only make you a boat
because I want to take that journey
back home where color dances under the moon
away from snow and my failing grades
the little groups we make, assuaging heart ache
my parents rusty dance once every month
in the graduate club with other transplanted souls
and the pair of ice skates I don't want for Xmas

I'm not from here, my heart is far away
I want to be with my friends in the sun
running under palms, drinking coconut water
taking our shirts off, diving into transparent water
not sitting here opposite you
hearing my mother with her new found accent

and short hair all pulled back
tell you I'm taking violin next semester
because you won't know why I chose music
or what my songs will be about
when I am old enough to sing them to a girl
she will have brown eyes and her ankles will click together
when she walks, it will be like love birds pecking
and you... pretty stranger making overtures

I will include you in a song
when I'm older back home
and done
being a little boy.

Doe a dear

Men with curled lips
like coiled bacon
sell drugs to girls in pleated miniskirts
school issue hiked up
something
feels dirty and lost
when driving off
in daddy's Jaguar
they snort and laugh
like young deer
blind in glare
unable to run
anywhere but
forward

Birthday card

My favorite birthday card
I never received
it thought of me
not on one day
marked by tradition
but ordinary mornings
uncharted
when
let down
raining
a child reaches
a girl strains
a woman holds her face
in reflection

how did she come to be?
here without knowing
how
bread crumbs in forest
message in a bottle
paint on stone
totems
for the seeker
sitting in old sunlight
trying to fit in
finds destination

a birthday
is not
gift, present, shiny coin
but being wanted
coming into caustic coil
those who celebrate
hold you
high
above broiling sea

It is within us

A house is not a home
to the fly who desperate for escape
roams
hitting glass in futile smear
no power of escape

we leave
returning to boxed memories
our old lives
scrapbooks and paste
it isn't the place
four walls and loud pipes
that gives us succor and keeps our hearts bright

a house is not a home
a fire on moor beckoning the weary
those attachments left in storybook
home is the advance of life
leaving who we were for who we become
shadows against sun
this beach
that stone
a way you smile at me
how fast our children grow
I carry in my belly, then my soul
home
a place of love
no walls
just your
warm hand
in mine

400 Breakups

Here are 400 breakups etched on my heart
I think
every time we do this
I will feel less hurt
and strangely
like paper cuts
like copper turns green and iron rusts
nothing feels less than
a literal rending
of all I am
without your
stabilizing star
I exist nowhere
this is just an outfit hanging in a closet
a face with no features
tongue speaking no language
eyes that cannot see through tears
somehow already years pass
even when I sleep

you see
I have squinted so long at the periphery of life
held up like Fat Tuesday crêpe
swollen with butter and milk
I don't move on my own
as if watching through your life
seeing my own
attached in felted pieces
patchworked to your ambition
speaking with your vision

I am
one of the dried damselflies I would
recoil from on my grandmothers windowsill
beautiful between apple blossoms until
in desiccation they reveal
an inner brittle, terrifyingly translucence
falling away like air eating air
never there

pulling up rhubarb, mixing bowls of custard
goldfinches heady with nectar beyond, she warned me as a child
put coconut oil on your scalp at night to keep from going bald
and I heard her hiding bottles behind the flatbacks at night

before sway took her to bed
nobody believed me then
I didn't learn to shout
but like the damson tree shaded by oak
I turned purple with setting sun

behind us, tiers of burnt fields
the fired smell of clay pigeons
sulphur from their sport
shoot for stars, everyone tried
except me
I preferred the dark
and that's where you found me
eating royal honey from a jar
my hair too long and split
by caustic other worlds, I hid then
In the sanctuary of your wings
thinking when you promised forever
It would be as the stream where I found my cat turning to bone
long it ran, never quitting, high into hills , heathered mauve
we would like branches intertwining
never let go

and now you are gone
I am
trying to start using my hands to make the shape of pain
such as it has shown in silhouette
itself, a fiery ache beneath dusty skin
where only you resided
where only you
I ever let so close

They

They ached to
cease
ritual so solidified
neither sure of exactly when
they first
sat
down
unable
to get up
ever again
the table scored with
knives run through in
war, come and gone
now
the dull insistent ring
of tinnitus replacing
light feet chasing
he's when she lives
beneath Sun
a golden thing he recalled
trying
despite the dryness of his skin
to form a smile in recollection
only breaking
surface
briefly
like old puppet
with worn
string
unable to
pull themselves
upright

Being Eddie Izzard

Client #54 said; h*as anyone ever told you look like Eddie Izzard?*
a female version … of course, she corrects, the implied insult hanging
like dog-whistling saliva caught on car door
maybe
coming from her world, a compliment, hard to tell
unreadable concrete eyes, disguising appetite
she's a cold heart, inhabiting a warm body
I'd say black heart but it seems racially charged, no longer gothic
her contrast comes when men, make her flower
she doesn't betray her longing for testosterone validation
says she wouldn't mind having casual sex like getting a massage
checking my reaction in the mirror of her shiny purse
not a raised eye-brow, not from this drag, she'll call late, asking for
compliments before climbing into Ambien night nurse
the best therapy transfers, unsaid longing, for distant fathers and cruel
mothers
fear of growing old, not being desired by men who feel gladdened to
mount so long as you're shaved and nubile
what will she become when she eclipses the age of her torment? She
never asks, but that's the question
and since I'm now a man, I could pat her knee, compliment her hair
she'll listen then, in a way women never listen with intensity, to a rival
if only I could tell her, I'm more interested in reading, than competing
perhaps I suit this particular illusion
of being Eddie Izzard

Candice Louisa Daquin has written poetry since childhood. Her early years were influenced by her grandparents who were artists and her memories of being a kid spending a lot of time displaced and transplanted, living in three different countries by her mid-twenties. Daquin grew up in Europe, the only child of intensely creative parents of Sephardic Jewish origin. Daquin's feeling of impermanence keenly influence her body of work and published her first poem at age 10 in a school magazine, before working on advertisements and modeling as a teen before studying at university. After her studies Daquin worked in the publishing industry, and spent many years sitting in the nose-bleed seats at live dance and ballet performances where she credits her inspiration and love of movement and dance.

Daquin moved to the USA in 2001, accidentally becoming part of the shift in America in terms of immigration and security post 9/11. It took her many years to settle during which time she wrote about her experiences as a foreigner at a time of heightened anxiety and tension. In the US Daquin pursued Psychotherapy and worked with families in several crisis centers before concentrating on teaching and writing full time. During a year in Canada, Daquin began writing reviews of poets and writers for magazines including *Rattle* and *The Northern Poetry Review*. Having written her own poetry and prose, Daquin was urged to publish her own work and her first collection of poetry; *A jar for the jarring* was published by STPG in 2015.

This was followed by three more books of poetry; Book Two: *The bright day has gone child and you are in for the dark* (TheFeatheredSleep Press, 2015) Book Three: *Illusions of existing* (TheFeatheredSleep Press, 2016) and Book Four: *Sit in fever* (TheFeatheredSleep Press, 2016). Additionally Daquin has been working on her first prose novel (a psychological thriller) and co-authored a limited edition book for her local jewish community called *#JeSuisJuif,* (TheFeatheredSleep Press, 2016) as well as mentoring fledgling writers to publish their work as part of her long standing belief of paying it forward.

Daquin's writing is uncompromising and raw, earning a large online following via her popular blog (www.thefeatheredsleep.com) where she has collaborated with other writers, most notably, contributing to the worldwide *Poets for Peace* collective poem and writing regularly for *Hijacked Amygdala* magazine. Her work has also been published by *Mansfield Press, Trivia: Voices of feminism, The Indiana Voice Magazine, The South Florida Poetry Journal, www.Ditchpoetry.com,* and *Memory House Magazine.*

Daquin brings her cultural and ethnic diversity to her writing focusing on themes such as; The experience of womanhood, alienation, societal prejudice, gender, immigration, taboos, mental health and transformation. In her spare time, Daquin loves vintage clothes, long walks, yoga, reading, dancing and geeking out on science magazines.

www.ingramcontent.com/pod-product-compliance
Lightning Source LLC
La Vergne TN
LVHW051611080426
835510LV00020B/3235